Three Dead Horses

Giving God the Reins

Marty Cosby

ISBN-13: 9798731677936
Library of Congress Control number: 2021906946

Cover Design – 100 Covers.com

Printed in the United States of American

Dedication

Dedication

To my Dad, the smartest and kindest man I have ever known. He was the most successful politician who never held an office. He taught me so much about life, especially how to treat people.

Ernie "Pete" Cosby

1936-2020

Three Dead Horses

Giving God the Reins

> *"Nearly all men can stand adversity, but if you want to test a man's character, give him power."*
>
> Abraham Lincoln

Contents

Acknowledgements

A lot of people made this book possible. Each one is worthy of a standing ovation:

My wife Sheliah, the love of my life and my biggest cheerleader. You have made this world a better place for me and everyone else.

My son Tyler. Your mother and I have been richly blessed since you came into our lives, over 30 years ago.

My mother. Growing up, my two brothers and I knew we were loved. Also, thank you for loving our dad.

Mike and Mitchell, my brothers who will tell anyone, *blood is thicker than water.*

Cathy Chumley, for being there with us and for us through it all. You never wavered.

Cindy Whitt, for your friendship.

Randy Bumgardner, for your encouragement and friendship.

Melissa Dishner, for your friendship, honesty, and prayers.

Ben Dishner, for your encouragement and prayers.

Steve and Trish Kyle, for your friendship over the past 30 years. You have been more like a brother and sister, and I love you both.

Gary and Rita McCann, for your honesty and friendship.

"It has been said that politics is the second oldest profession. I have learned that it bears a striking resemblance to the first."

Ronald Reagan

Introduction

You prepare a table before me in the presence of my enemies;
You have anointed my head with oil; My cup overflows.
Psalm 23:5 (NASB)

Seasons come and go. Some of them go by too quickly while others stay around longer than we would like. One of the longest seasons in my life was from April 2016-May 2017. I thought the sun would never breach the dark clouds of despair that seemed to linger for an eternity. During this time my faith was shaken to the core. I know God uses trials and sufferings to mold us in the image of his Son; but I have to admit, it almost got the best of me.

God used this time to teach me three lessons for which I am now most grateful. He also used this trial to remind me of what is really important in life; the things that truly matter. Somewhere along the way I had lost sight of this.

I had taken God's blessings in my life for granted: time spent with my parents and the comfort and security of my childhood home, the feeling I got when my son looked at me and thought I hung the moon (although far from the truth, I let him think it), waking up every morning next to the woman of my dreams, and the beauty of a sunrise.

It was almost as if God picked me up by the shirt collar and gave me a really good shaking and said, *"Look at what you have - a family that loves you, a family that is proud of you, and that will stand with you. Look at your Blessings! Wake Up!"*

Before God jolted me back into reality, I did throw myself the biggest pity party I could afford. I invited my closest friends at the time – Misery, Depression, and Fear. I mingled with Misery, drank cocktails with Depression, and flirted with Fear. It was some party. Satan was there, too. Although I didn't invite him, he was there with bells on. I can hear him now, encouraging Misery to taste the hors d'oeuvres of Misfortune, telling Depression to dance the night away with Despair and suggesting that the fretful cocktail Fear held in her hand needed to be refilled.

A year before, I had just finished my twentieth year as principal of a small rural county school in East Tennessee. I started my career as an educator at this same school in the fall of 1981 as a special education teacher. I was asked to teach computer classes eleven years later before becoming principal in 1995. During my twenty years as a school principal, my dream job, I was fortunate and blessed with a unique and very special situation. During those twenty years I worked with my wife and father.

No, before you ask, I did not hire either one. My dad, head of maintenance, was there first. I was hired three years later and my wife was hired seven years later as an eighth-grade teacher. When I became principal the county did not have a nepotism policy in place. So, we were all allowed to stay at the school.

An ideal situation?

Probably not.

But it worked for us. They never expected preferential treatment, and they never received it. The director of schools at the time, called my wife and asked her to come by his office one afternoon before I was hired. They were friends, and his wife had been her mentor. His only question was, "Will it be a problem having your husband as your boss?" Not wanting to hurt my chances at a promotion, she thought for a second and responded, "Well, he would only be my boss at work." They both laughed at her reply as she blushed. He told her that I would make a great principal.

During my tenure as principal I was named as one of Tennessee's most effective principals two times, once in 2007 and again in 2009. Also, in 2009 I was inducted into the Educators' Hall of Fame at my Alma Mater, Lincoln Memorial University. In 2010 I was named East Tennessee Field Representative Principal of the Year, which covered sixteen East Tennessee counties; and in 2015 I was named Tennessee Education Association Administrator of the Year. I mention the above achievements, in no way to boast. I do mention them to prove a point.

Located in northeast Tennessee about fifty miles from Knoxville, along the borders of Kentucky and Virginia, our county never had a shortage on small town politics and corruption. It seemed every job depended on how many votes you can influence.

If you want to keep your job you are expected to stay on the right side of politics. It doesn't matter what kind of job you do or how hard you work...the only thing that matters is who you know or how many votes you can sway. That is the point I want to make – Politics is more important than doing a good job. How many votes you can influence is more important to some elected officials than preparing our students for the future.

Having tenure as a teacher can serve as some protection from corrupt, greedy school board members. Acquiring tenure can protect a job, but usually not a position. In the state of Tennessee principals do not have tenure as a principal, but they can have tenure as a teacher. While it is unfortunate that tenure does protect incompetence and immorality at times, it can also protect you from unethical behaviors of school board members that must be kept in check. When left unchecked, innocent men and women are hurt and sometimes destroyed.

Now, this is not a story about losing a job or being transferred to a different position. But it does start there – actually it starts a little earlier - with me exercising my right to vote the way I choose and choosing not to play politics.

This story is about power and corruption in a small East Tennessee county. It is a story about how ruthless politicians and unethical school leaders tried to destroy my family and me when I stood up to them. They even used tax dollars to do it.

Most importantly, this is a story about God's love, mercy, and guidance through the darkest time of my life. I will share with

17

you lessons He taught me and how He blessed me and my family

in the presence of our enemies!

> *"The greater your knowledge of the goodness and grace of God on your life, the more likely you are to praise Him in the storm."*
>
> Matt Chandler

Chapter 1

Three Dead Horses

"However, there is a God in heaven who reveals mysteries, and He has made known to King Nebuchadnezzar what will take place in the latter days. This was your dream and the visions in your mind while on your bed.

Daniel 2:28

Thursday night

July 21, 2016

I had no clue where I was at first. I tried hard to recognize the place that surrounded me, but I was unable. I felt confused.

Where am I?

I shut my eyes and reopened them. I was standing in the middle of an old country road. There were no cars, the sun had set, and the air had a chill to it. The smell of freshly cut grass filled the air.

I tried to move from the middle of the road, but my legs were weak and heavy. I finally trudged to the shoulder of the road with my lethargic limbs as waves of questions, confusion and anxiety crashed into me.

Where am I?

How did I get here?

What am I doing here alone?

Where is my family?

Does my presence on this untenanted road in the middle of nowhere have anything to do with the threats that my family and I had been receiving? I wondered. I couldn't say I had not been warned. Oh no, I was warned. Warned by the corrupt individuals I stood against and cautioned by my family and friends. But these crooked politicians who hid behind a title and sometimes religion, preyed on both young and old, and they needed to be stopped or at least exposed.

My new spot in the road brought into focus a building that sat on a slight hill just above the ditch.

Wait!

I recognize this building.

That is why the road seemed familiar. The building – an old country store.

My mother and father used to shop at this very store when I was a young boy.

Memories of my childhood flooded my mind as I savored the overwhelming smell of the old country store where my mother and father bought supplies and groceries. My mother would always make sure my two brothers and I got our favorite candy on every trip. My brothers would each get a pack of *Kings* candy cigarettes and an *Oh Henry* candy bar. For me it would be a box of *Red Hots* cinnamon candy and a box of *Crackerjacks*.

The aroma of candy, leather, tobacco, coffee and musty

oiled wooden floors all would meet you when you entered the door. I recall how the shelves behind the counters and around the walls were stacked with everything from canned goods to clothing.

I remember my dad would get a couple pairs of *Pointer Brand* bib overalls each year when the tobacco crop sold. My mom would buy my two brothers and me school clothes and shoes with tobacco crop income. She occasionally would get a new dress and a pair of shoes for herself.

Groceries and supplies with extended shelf life were also purchased with tobacco crop income. Other items were purchased and charged to an in-store account as needed. The tobacco income would settle the charges from one year to the next. We grew most of our food, so the charges were minimal. The country store was the hub of our community in the 1960s and early 70s.

In the center of the store sat a pot-bellied stove

surrounded by four wooden chairs, a coal bucket filled with coal, a

box of split wood and a checkerboard atop an empty pickle barrel

for the old timers' entertainment during winter months. I thought

of my grandfather and how he was the self-proclaimed checker

champion of the community five years in a row. It was around

that pot-belly stove that I would listen to my dad and others talk

about an array of subjects from the Bible to the weather. But the

subject I enjoyed most was politics. I have always been intrigued

with the affairs of government, especially local government.

There were many times the discussion of politics would get as hot

as the potbelly stove they surrounded.

The old timers would move to the outside as the weather

warmed up. Their favorite pass time was whittling in the warmer

months. They never carved anything in particular – they just kept

whittling until the piece of cedar was gone. I guess, looking back,

it was therapeutic in a way - watching their worries and difficulties

fall to the floor to be swept away later, as the piece of fragrant

evergreen disappeared.

I thought about the first knife my dad bought me at this very store, as a wave of nostalgia washed over me. My grandfather taught me how to hold the *Barlow* knife as I tried whittling for the first time. Closing my eyes again and taking a deep breath - I could smell fresh cedar shavings.

WAIT!! WAIT!!

That old store has been closed for years. Abandoned. Deserted. Forsaken.

I open my eyes.

Am I dreaming?

Yes I have to be dreaming. The old mercantile had not been in business for over 40 years. The aroma of the cedar shavings and oiled wooden floors vanished.

The chill in the air turned ice cold as I got a whiff of a gross noxious odor coming from the culvert. Much like the nauseating, disgusting stench of dirty politicians who prey on the poor and helpless. In this county, as in so many across the country, corruption had no bounds. You name it – kickbacks, bid-rigging, drugs, rape. Our county has had its fair share of sleaziness among elected officials.

Something catches my eye in the ditch below the old dilapidated, ramshackle of a building that used to regale reigning checker champions. I move closer to the edge of the road to get a better look.

I jumped back and covered my nose at what I saw and smelled.

Horses.

Dead horses!

Three of them.

One horse silver in color, one copper-red and the third black.

All three lifeless and bloody. It was clear they had been

slaughtered. What other explanation could there be? Each horse wore a brown hand tooled leather saddle drenched in blood.

More questions saturated my thoughts. My thinking was not clear.

Who massacred the horses?

Was this a warning to me and my family that we had better drop legal actions against the corrupt individuals of the county?

If this is a dream, it just turned into a nightmare.

Startled by the sound of footsteps on squeaky wooden steps I looked up to see someone walking up the steps of the old store. The building again appeared as it was when I was a young boy. Nothing rickety about the building now. The aroma of oiled wooden floors and leathery tobacco once again filled the night air.

I didn't recognize the person standing on the steps. More questions pounded my already hurting head.

Why am I here?

Where is my family? I must find them.

Who is the person on the steps that keeps watching me?

Maybe he knows where my wife and son are.

Why are these horses here?

Why are they dead?

Who killed them?

The shadowy enigmatic figure on the steps summoned me to come near the building.

I hesitated.

I needed to distance myself - I must distance myself from the redolence of death but wondered if I could trust the stranger that beckoned me to join him.

Why would I trust him?

Or was it a her?

Maybe this individual, whoever he or she is, is the one that slaughtered the horses. That's it! He slaughtered the horses as they grazed in the little green patch of grass just above the road and dumped each of them in the ditch.

But why? None of this makes any sense!

All I want to do is locate my family and go home. I don't like this place. It's not the same as it was when I was younger. I remember thinking again I need to get away from the sickening, **disgusting, odor** that again floated up from the ditch. The odor became stronger and stronger.

The mysterious stranger beckoned me to come to him again. Perhaps he plans on me being his next victim. Or maybe, he knows where my family is and wants to take me to them. If he has information about my family...I have to find out what he knows.

I wondered again -

Can I trust whoever this is?

Do I have a choice?

I have to find my family. I am not leaving without them.

I started walking toward the mysterious being that was now on the top step and facing me. The closer I got to him the more I wanted to be home, but I was not leaving until I was back with my family.

Slowly and cautiously, moving toward the mysterious stranger, I felt my legs become lifeless and heavy again. It feels as if I had just been submerged in a quagmire.

I began thinking this is it!

I'm not going to live! I am going to drown in this sticky, nasty, black sludge.

Each step became more and more demanding as the wet, sticky muck oozed from my shoes. I found it difficult to breathe. What am I doing in this filth? The odor from the dead horses became unbearable.

I started to pray.

I prayed for God to end this nightmare and reunite me with my wife and son. I didn't care how he did it - I just wanted to be out of this terrifying and confusing place.

As I approached the old store, I heard the flight of steps begin squeaking. The mysterious person walking toward me with an outstretched hand said, "Let me help you."

With both feet out of the mire and planted on the bottom step of the old building that use to be a thriving supplier of necessities, I demanded to know his identity. He smiled and said, "Come with me and I will watch over you."

I turned and looked at the marshland I had just waded through, with each murky step thinking it could be my last. I had to cover my mouth and nose to keep from vomiting from the stench that still lingered in the night air. I turned back to the stranger, who appeared to be in no hurry - still waiting patiently for my decision.

I take one step toward the flight of steps and notice lights coming on in the building. With the next step the front door opens, and the aroma of **oiled wooden floors and leathery tobacco and cinnamon candy replaces the** stench that ascended from the ditch just a few feet away.

Not fully understanding why I had a yearning to trust this person - I wasn't even sure I had another choice. I was tired and frightened and needed to locate my family. With each seized step, I started feeling more and more at ease. I couldn't explain it or what I was feeling, but I was terrified and felt safe at the same time. As a wave of emotions washed over me, somehow I knew everything was going to be okay.

> *"Power does not corrupt. Fear corrupts... perhaps the fear of a loss of power."*
>
> John Steinbeck

Chapter 2

Political Incest

When the righteous increase, the people rejoice, But when a wicked man rules, people groan.

- Proverbs 29:2 NASB

He got straight to the point with his call. He didn't say "hello" or "how are you". He just started barking. Small talk was never his forte, but giving orders was. The two things he enjoyed most was ordering people around and talking about himself. He enjoyed telling everyone, who cared to listen, how the county was thriving under his management and how the county school system was excelling under his leadership. He never provided any proof when he was grandstanding. Very seldom was he ever called into question about those claims. When someone did dare to disagree with him on anything he claimed, he always gave a strawman response. He was very good at distracting the public and distorting the facts.

One night at a school board meeting as he pushed an energy proposal on the rest of the school board, claiming it would save the school system hundreds of thousands of dollars, another board member asked, *How it would save money and how much it would cost the system upfront?* He went on defense and accused this other board member of not wanting the teachers and students to have a warm place to teach and learn. (It was rumored there were kickbacks on this energy proposal).

All he had to do to hang on to his school board seat was keep the 6th district happy. Keeping the seven-member finance committee content was the key to holding his position as director of finance.

Holding the seat of a school board member, an elected position and county financial director, an appointed position, presents a powerful position. When the same person holds both positions at the same time, there is an enormous conflict of interest.

Financial directors in Tennessee counties are appointed by a finance committee made up of seven members. In our county, the finance committee consists of the county mayor, director of schools, supervisor of highways, and four members of the legislative body, which are county commissioners.

Conflict of interest catches the eye when the school board votes on a director of school's contract, and the director of schools votes on a financial director's contract.

You scratch by back, and I'll scratch yours.

Political Incest.

When a school board member calls a principal of a school, it usually means one of two things. Either they have had a complaint from a constituent, or they want their *back scratched*. Sometimes it is both.

He was not modest in his demand. His exact words were, "I want you to get your family together this weekend. Sit them down and tell them they are voting for the incumbent this year for mayor." Everyone knew he and the incumbent had scratched each other's back for the past four years. And now he wanted me to scratch an itch that the incumbent mayor couldn't reach, and I just wasn't willing to get my hands dirty.

My response to his pressure took me a little by surprise. I have always been respectful of school board members. It was not a secret, that employment placement depended on them. I mean, an employee did not want to upset the members of a school board for fear of ending up working in a position or location they didn't want or like.

My response was, "No, that is not going to happen. I will decide who to vote for, and my family will do the same." His reply to my refusal took me a little by surprise as well, although it shouldn't have. He told me I didn't have a choice in the matter.

I don't have a choice in the matter!

Are you kidding me?

I started to wonder if I had even heard him right. My head

started to spin and hurt. It was not yet 8 o'clock, and I was dealing with idiocy like this. I asked the next three things that came to my mind, not giving him time to answer before I asked the next question.

"Did you just tell me I did not have a choice in the matter?"

"What does that mean?"

"Are you kidding me?"

"I don't kid around when it comes to matters like this!" he growled. I wanted to ask him, "Who do you think you are?" But I decided not to, realizing he had drawn a line in the sand and I had stepped across it. I asked him why the election of this mayor was that important to him. Although I knew the answer, I guess I really wanted to hear him to say it. I wanted to hear him say that he needed the mayor's support and vote to keep his job as financial director.

Sure enough, the next thing that came out of mouth was, "I don't have time to break in another mayor. Our county is doing great, we are saving money, and taxes have not been raised in years. The mayor is listening to me. He is doing what I tell him. And I really don't have the time to train another person for Mayor. And if he doesn't win this election my job as financial director could be in jeopardy."

He also said something else that was interesting. He told me that this certain mayor got into financial trouble just a year or so before he was elected and had to file bankruptcy. He told me that a prominent county businessperson bankrolled his campaign and the bankroller was wanting their money with interest. The only way they would get their money was if the mayor kept his $100,000 a year job.

I did not ask who the bankroller was. I knew. Most everyone in the county did. "Don't you only need four votes from the finance committee to extend your contract?" I asked, knowing the answer. "Yes," he said, "I have the road commissioner and two county commissioners. The director of schools will only vote for me if I need her vote or if I am the only one they are voting on.

We decided it would look better that way since I vote on her job."

"Wow," I thought. That's small-town politics at its best or worst.

You scratch my back and I'll scratch yours. Quid pro quo.

"Well, maybe you can sway one or both of the other two county commissioners - or tell the director of schools how to vote, but I am not voting for the incumbent."

He repeated his directive for me to get my family together and tell them how to vote. He said, "I will get with you next week for an update."

The next thing I heard was a loud CLICK.

Are you kidding me?

My head started pounding now.

Did he not hear what I said? I guess not, I told myself.

Was he not listening when I verbalized, "No that is not going to happen. I will decide who to vote for, and my family will do the same."

He's going to get with me next week for an update?

I sat at my desk for 20 minutes without moving after I heard the "click".

I felt numb. Dazed. A little disoriented.

What were my options?

Do I have any?

Still a little confused, I tried to make sense of the last few minutes. Although it seemed to have lasted more than an hour, it was only a ten-minute conversation. He did draw a line in the sand, and I crossed it. Or did I draw the line? Either way I crossed a line with a narcissistic individual who had a lot of power in the county. There would be consequences. I was sure of that.

❧

As a school principal, being accountable for all facets of my school, I wore different hats throughout any given day. Hats of a mediator, a disciplinarian, a curriculum specialist, a budget expert, public relations adviser and on and on. The job is both demanding and rewarding; but with the added harassment of corrupt school boards and politicians, it was unbearable at times.

I thought for a fleeting moment he would not call back and I could forget about his banter. But that notion faded as I remembered this is the same person that is **alleged** to have run for school board so he could fire a popular elementary basketball coach for not starting his son on the team.

Vindictiveness, malice and retaliation should not have a seat on the school board. But sadly, people do run for office just to get even with someone. When people run for office such as school board to settle a score and get elected, students, teachers and taxpayers suffer.

I will get with you next week for an update.

What kind of update? Did he want an update on how my

family responded to his demand? An update on how closely I followed his orders? No doubt he will be after both.

It was Wednesday of the following week before he called. The call was short and to the point. He didn't ask how things were going at the school, or if I needed anything to help perform my job. He didn't ask how the students or teachers were doing. I actually would have been surprised if he had.

"Did you talk with your mom and dad and your brothers over the weekend?" he asked. I told him I did visit with my parents over the weekend, but my brothers were not there.

"Fine, fine but you need to call them tonight and get them on board." I still wondered what he heard when I told him, that is not going to happen. Without skipping a beat he asked, "Are your parents on board?"

I took a deep breath and told him we would not be bullied into voting for someone we didn't believe was capable of doing the job. I also asked him what he meant last week when he said I didn't have a choice. In a condescending tone he said, "What part of that statement do you not understand?"

He went on to say, "All you need to do is stay out of the election, vote the way I say and everything will be fine. Otherwise things will not work out for you and you can remember I told you so."

Obviously, who won the county mayor's race was very important to him, but it was also important to him for people to obey him. It was like he got a high from people bowing down to him and following his demands. He actually told me that I was making him look bad in the county. When I asked him how, he said he had promised supporters of the incumbent that he could get my family to also support him.

A round of profanity exploded like fireworks when I told him that he shouldn't make promises he cannot keep. After the obscenities' finale he told me without catching his breath, "You have been warned! You and your family have betrayed all of us, and it will not end well for you!"

CLICK

Betrayed all of us.

Who is *all of us*? How did we betray them? What was he

talking about? What did he mean?

I thought, I really need to stop stepping over lines drawn in

the sand. In the months and years of turmoil that followed, I have

been asked more than once why I just didn't go vote and say I

voted for the incumbent. I know that would have saved a lot of

grief, but at the end of the day I have to live with myself. Besides,

I don't like being intimidated and harassed by these corrupt

politicians.

> *"Politicians are like diapers, they need to be changed often, and for the same reasons."*
>
> *Mark Twain*

Chapter 3

Birds of a Feather

First of all, then, I urge that entreaties and prayers,
petitions and thanksgivings, be made on behalf of all men, for
kings and all who are in authority, so that we may lead a tranquil
and quiet life in all godliness and dignity.

1 Timothy 2:1-2 (NASB)

Elections in our county have never failed to entertain the voters. Boredom never cast a shadow on inhabitants of our county during election years. As a youngster I would listen to attention-grabbing stories about county politics and the corruption that seeped from county officials like moonshine from a seasoned still which was eventually traded for votes. Elders, sitting around a potbelly stove at the local country store discussed each race in detail and argued over who would win and why they were going to vote for or against certain candidates.

On one particular occasion I vividly remember my grandfather laughing and slapping his knee as he said, *"The sheriff's race would have been a lot closer this year had the dead*

not voted," while wiping tobacco juice from his chin with the back

of his hand. As a young boy it was a mystery to me how a dead

person could vote, but I held my questions until later when I had

my grandfather's full attention. Recalling the old-timers' accounts

of county politics, I realize that watching and telling stories were

both a source of entertainment and relief during difficult

economic times.

One of my favorite stories growing up listening to tales

around that potbellied stove was about "Boss Maples" and the

1942 general election for county judge/mayor. I must have heard

that story a hundred times. That election, like so many others,

was infused with fraud and misconduct. The '42 election unseated

the incumbent county judge (now called mayor), but he refused

to relinquish the office after a Supreme Court ruled the election

invalid because of voter fraud. Evidence showed the successful

candidate contributed money to a slush fund to the tune of more

than $6,000 which was used illegally for the purchase of poll tax receipts and for influencing voters. At one of the larger precincts, an election commissioner, also acting as one of the judges, permitted and assisted more than 100 people to vote illegally, marking their ballots when they were not physically disabled and buying votes.

A well-known businessman and tavern owner was appointed to hold the election at another of the larger county precincts. He purchased several hundred poll tax receipts and on the day of the election, took the ballot box at gun point to his business and, according to the testimony of some of the witnesses, ordered everybody out of the room. When he later returned the ballot box it was determined by the court that it was not the same one he had removed earlier.

In this same election "Boss Maples" voted for the first and last time. "Boss" was said to have been smart, friendly and high-spirited. The ladies loved him and called him adorable while the men...well, they called him their "best friend." Yes, you probably guessed it.... "Boss Maples" aka "Boss the Hound" was a well-known coon dog in the area.

As a young boy I wondered how in the world dead people and a coon dog could mark a ballot and why they were allowed to do so.

 A court ruling rendered the 1942 county election incurably uncertain after it was determined violations of the law and safeguards surrounding the balloting had been ignored.   The defendant was taxed with the costs.

Today's campaign seasons still entertain the voters. As political signs begin to sprout early in the election season, strange bedfellows begin to grow. Candidates make deals with candidates and double-cross others. Oftentimes, citizens end up paying the price for deals and dishonesty with less services and inadequate infrastructure. Citizens with little or no influence also pay the price by not having a voice.

When the 2014 election rolled into town not much had changed except the players. At the beginning of the election I was told how I would be voting on a certain mayoral candidate and that my family would be voting the same way. I was told in no uncertain terms to stay out of the election, vote the way I was told and everything will be fine. Otherwise things will not work out for me. When I refused to be a puppet for the county puppet master, the intimidation and harassment began.

My family and I attended a "meet and greet" for an opposing mayoral candidate in early May of 2014. We were there to listen to his viewpoints and learn more about his plan to move our county forward. The next day the school board member/finance director called my office. I was not surprised by the call. What surprised me was what he said. "I have a list of people that attended the event last night, you know, *the meet and greet,* your candidate held. And you and a lot of your family members are on the list," he stated.

Wow. I thought.

Is this what we have come to?   Taking names.

Did he just admit that he had someone spying on us?

"I told you to stay out of the election and vote the way I say and you will have nothing to worry about. Things are not going to work out for you if you don't," he scolded.

Although it was early in the election season, I was getting weary with the **intimidation and harassment. Little did I know, the worst was yet to come.**

※

My thoughts flashed back again to my childhood and the old country store. I remember my dad, grandfather and community members discussing a variety of topics and exchanging stories around a pot-belly stove. No matter what topics they discussed, you could count on **politics** being part of the array. A lot of the times politics was the only topic covered.

It was not uncommon for politicians to visit the country store or our family farm specifically to talk with my dad and get his support for their campaign. Every election hopeful candidates would make it a point to come by seeking my dad's guidance and backing. My dad was known throughout the county for giving sound and honest political advice. Candidates were told if they wanted to be successful, they needed to garner the support of Ernie "Pete" Cosby.

Even after elections were over and the votes counted, the winners came by to pick my dad's brain. School board members, sheriffs, and commissioners to name a few, would pay my dad a visit on a regular basis to say thank you and seek his advice.

So, when the master manipulator wanted my family to support his candidate I understood why. People respected my dad and wanted his support, but we could not back his contender for several reasons. The biggest reason - we did not feel that the candidate had the ability to move our county forward.

He had already served four years as county mayor, and no progress had been made. We were not moving forward as a county; our job market was stagnant. We needed a leader with a vision. We needed someone who was not controlled by the established *good ol' boys club*. The *good ol' boys club* would meet most every day at the same restaurant, same time, same table. That table became the unofficial county seat, with the finance director presiding over the business.

The harassment and threats continued.

Out in the open!

One evening some of my family members and I attended a mayoral debate hosted by the local university. We sat with the candidate's family during the debate that we had decided to support. I know - we don't take orders well.

I noticed the master manipulator staring our way most of the evening. I tried to convince myself that it was my imagination but I was proven wrong when he came up to me after the debate and stuck his finger in my face and said, "You will regret this!"

Standing around discussing the events of the evening with some of my family and friends after the debate had wrapped up, I noticed the finance director briskly walking toward us. I tried not to make eye contact with him. The closer he got, the more uncomfortable I became. His face was as red as the bag of Grainger County tomatoes a friend had brought my dad that evening. His shirt was soaked with perspiration from the humidity of the evening and the humiliation from some of the answers his candidate delivered.

When asked about transparent government the finance director's candidate said, "There is nothing being transparent around our county. There's nothing transparent; I promise you that it's all public record." I wished I could have pressed pause and rewind - just to make sure I had heard him correctly. But chuckles from the audience told me that I had. One of my brothers looked my way and grinned when the *nothing in our county is transparent* statement was made from the platform.

The threats and intimidation continued throughout the 2014 county election. We were told if we attended any more functions for any candidate other than the one he wanted us to support, we would be making a grave mistake. One from which we would not be able to recover. We would receive as many as two or three threatening letters a week outlining how things were going to change for us after the election if we didn't get on board. I was also told my family was letting everyone down and that we would be the laughing stock of the entire county when all this is over. The letters were never signed but most ended with – *You can remember I told you so!*

"The only thing worse than a liar is a liar that's also a hypocrite!"

Tennessee Williams

Chapter 4

Read Between The Lies

There are six things that the Lord hates, seven that are an abomination to him: haughty eyes, a lying tongue, and hands that shed innocent blood, a heart that devises wicked plans, feet that make haste to run to evil, a false witness who breathes out lies, and one who sows discord among brothers.

-Proverbs 6:17-19

It was like being kicked in the gut. Her words hit hard enough to knock the wind from my soul.

"Why would you do this?" "Why would you transfer her?" "What has she done?" knowing my wife had done nothing wrong.

The director of schools answer..."I don't have a choice. I have to. I'm being forced to. My hands are tied."

A deafening silence filled the room. It was so piercing it forced her to speak again. "You know how a certain school board member is when he doesn't get his way. You refused to play his games and now he's got it in for you."

"But why her? She has done nothing to deserve being jerked around like this."

"I agree. She is a good teacher, but she is your wife, and he wants to send your family a message. Be glad it's not you being jerked round. He wanted you transferred. Actually, he wants me to do more than transfer you."

Be glad it's not me being jerked around. Seriously?

"When someone mistreats my wife they mistreat me," I said almost yelling.

"She is not being mistreated, she still has a job!" Her tone was one of annoyance mixed with sarcasm.

"Actually, he wanted me to do a lot more to you than transfer you, but I convinced him that transferring your wife would send the same massage. That seemed to make him happy."

Her words sent chills down my spine.

That seemed to make him happy.

Making a school board member happy is more important than the students?

Making a school board member happy is more important than the way you treat people?

It was at that moment I knew she had sold her soul to the corruption that has plagued our county for as long as I can remember. Political corruption, small town politics, whatever you choose to call, it is an evil that is difficult to annihilate. It eats away at the soul of a community.

"What you are doing is wrong both morally and legally," I shouted again. "We will fight this," I said.

She walked behind her cluttered desk, pulled out a chair and sat down. Folding her arms she said, "Look, you need to go with this and learn to live with it. Otherwise things could get messy for you."

I couldn't believe what I as hearing.

Things could get messy for me.

"That sounds like a threat to me. And I don't like being threatened," I said almost yelling as I headed to the door. She said, "Either get with the plan, or I will move you to another school and tell everyone you were insubordinate." I turned to face her. I asked the only thing that came to my mind at the time, "You would tell a bald-faced lie?" As soon as that question came out of my mouth, I said under my breath, "Of course you would."

I could tell the *bald-face lie* question had infuriated her. Her tone went from annoyance and sarcasm to anger and frustration. "It is not a lie!" she yelled. "I'm telling you...NO, I'M ORDERING you to get on board with this decision, or I will write you up as insubordinate and move you to another school."

I really couldn't believe what I was hearing again.

"You can't punish me for not going along with something illegal." Or could she? I was confused. My family had been harassed and threatened for over a year now, and I really didn't know how much more we could take. With a smug and self-

righteous look more venom spewed from her month, "I'm the

director of schools and you will do as you are told. Now leave!"

The 2014 election was in the books and I just wanted

things to get back normal. But the director of schools admitted

that the finance director wanted to send my family a message.

The message – *YOU DID NOT OBEY ME - SO NOW YOU HAVE TO*

PAY. MAYBE NEXT TIME YOU WILL DO AS YOU ARE TOLD.

The finance director's candidate for mayor won the

election, and there were loose ends that needed to be tied up. My

family being at the top of the list.

When I got home and told my wife about the encounter

with the director of schools, I could tell she was hurt, but not

surprised. I told her that we would fight the injustice and that I

believed we had a good chance of winning.

The next morning, we placed a call to the Tennessee Education Association and explained the events that led up to my wife being transferred. In two days a TEA representative and my wife were meeting with the director of schools in her office.

My wife said the meeting began with the TEA representative stating that it is believed this teacher's recent transfer was politically motivated. We just want to hear your side and give you a chance to explain why she was transferred so we can clear up any confusion there may be.

After a long pause a layer of tension settled in the room, the director started by saying, "I transferred her because I need her expertise. The school that I transferred her to is struggling with K-4 literacy. She is an expert in the field of literacy." The TEA representative asked the director if she had discussed the transfer with my wife. The director said, "Maybe, I'm not sure, but I did tell her husband and he was on board with it."

The TEA representative said, "So you are saying this

teacher has done nothing wrong. And the only reason she was transferred is because you needed her expertise at another school."

"She absolutely has not done anything wrong," was her reply. "She is one of the best teachers in the county, and she has a lot to offer," she said with a syrupy sweet voice. The TEA representative then asked, "So, you want to place her in a position of K-4 literacy when she has no experience at all in K-4."

My wife told me the director looked confused and agitated. The director asked, "What do you mean?" Our representative explained herself, "Well, you told us that the reason she was transferred was that you needed her expertise at this K-4 school. The fact is she has spent her entire career with middle school students. She has no expertise in K-4." My wife said the blood appeared to drain from the director's face as it turned pale white, then blood red.

Her next statement was, "Let me pray about this," as she

glanced at the TEA representative then at my wife and then down at her hands which were folded tightly on her desk. The TEA representative asked when they could expect to hear from her about a decision? Getting up from her desk and moving toward the door she said, "In a day or two."

Three days later the director called my cell while I was having lunch at Puckett's Restaurant, in Nashville, with our school's Beta club. Ironically I was in Nashville accepting an Administrator of the Year Award from The Tennessee Education Association. When I saw it was her calling, I excused myself from the table and went outside so we could talk. While I was standing on the corner of 5th and Church Street, she told me that she was going to reverse my wife's transfer, but since I would not get on board she was moving me to another school. "Why would you do this?" I asked. "I just told you that you refused to get with the plan, and now, you have to pay the price," she said.

I could feel a slithering sadness begin to penetrate my soul. I felt that the situation was becoming hopeless as frustration followed the sadness. The only thing that would come out of my wounded being was, "You know I will fight this." I wanted to say more. I needed to say more. I wanted to ask a lot more questions. But I wasn't able. The wind had been knocked from my spirt.

She said with an arrogant tone, "I thought you might."

I started my fight by calling the same TEA representative that went to bat for my wife. She got a meeting with the director of schools in less than two weeks. She started by saying that it is believed this recent transfer was politically motivated. Can you tell me why he was transferred? The director said with a smile, "He is an outstanding principal, and is phenomenal with young children. We need his nurturing skills at this new school."

I asked, "Have I done anything wrong?" I wanted her answer to be on record. "Honey, you know I think you are doing a good job at your school. But I need your loving and nurturing skills at your new placement," she said. With each of her double words, I wondered if she could taste the depravity that oozed from her lips.

Although it was on record that I had done nothing wrong, it didn't make me feel any better. How in the world could she sit there and let the lies roll off her tongue like water from a faucet? I wanted to vomit. I wanted to ask her more question, but I knew if I did everyone in the room would know what I had for lunch.

The TEA representative asked if she would consider transferring me back since I only wanted to work one more year and then retire. I had spent my entire career at the same school and would have preferred a different ending. The director of schools looked my way and smiled.

Was she smiling because she was rubbing it in? She knew that I knew she was lying. Or had she had a change of heart? Was she ready to lay down the dirty politics and play by the rules? Was she ready to do her job as director?

Her next statement confused me even more. Still smiling she said, "Let me pray about this." Yes she really said she wanted to pray about the situation. The TEA representative advised, "Let's give her a few days. Who knows, she changed her mind about your wife. Maybe she will about you as well."

In the meeting nothing was discussed about insubordination or not *going along with the plan*. I'm not sure it would have mattered. With the outside chance she had a change of heart I didn't want to risk another change of heart. I took the advice of the TEA representative and waited. It did not take her long to get back to me with her decision. She called and told me after she had prayed she has decided to stick with her original plan and transfer me to another school.

A line had been crossed, and I was in new territory. I didn't know how to handle things. I felt I had to stop what was happening to me and my family. I needed to take a stand, so after a lot of prayer and advise I took legal action. A decision I did not enter into lightly.

The director of schools gave a different reason for the transfer each time she was asked. None of the reasons were factual or based on any shred of truth. She gave conflicting answers to me and the TEA representative two weeks following the transfer. She even admitted that I had done nothing wrong. She gives a different reason in the depositions, and yet another different reason in the affidavit attached to the motion for summary judgment.

To connect to the dots - I mean the lies.

- June 2015, the director of schools told me and a Tennessee Education Association representative that she transferred me because my nurturing skills were needed at the new school.

- In her deposition, taken in May of 2017 the director states that she had no other problems with me or my performance other than the alleged insubordination:

Q. Okay. Up until this issue of him being transferred from his school to other school, you had not any complaints or issues with Mr. Cosby in the past, had you?

A. The insubordination bothered me. But other than that, no.

- In her sworn affidavit dated May 22, 2018 the director

  stated, "he was transferred for other reasons."

  Her reasons: *His school was performing poorly on state-mandated tests, as determined by the Tennessee Department of Education. Leadership was needed at that school to achieve higher student performance on mandated test. The school Mr. Cosby was being transferred to would benefit from his leadership in the role of a nurturer to younger children."*

In March of 2015, an entire two months before the state test were even administered, the director approached another principal in the county about moving her to my school so she could move me. See transcript from deposition below:

"Q: All right. Do you recall a conversation where the director, came to you and told you she was going to have

to move Mr. Cosby somewhere and asked if you would consider coming to his school so she could place Mr. Cosby to your school in March 2015?

A. Yes. I went to her. She didn't come to me.
Q. All right. Tell me about that.

A. I got a phone call from her secretary, asking if I could come by central office that afternoon, and I went by.

The director admits this is an accurate reflection of the conversation, and that I would not be at my school in March of 2015, an entire month before the test were even administered:

Q. [The director], you did discuss Mr. Cosby's employment with another principal?

A. Yes, sir.

Q. You understand that under the code of ethics that you're not supposed to do that?

A. I didn't discuss -- I asked her if she was interested in going to his school. So because I asked her if she was interested in going to his school as the principal then -- I mean, she understood that he would not be there.

It would be impossible for the director to know that my school would have poor test scores in March of 2015, when she admitted I would not be there unless she planned to purposely alter the test before they were sent to the state for recording in an order

to sabotage my record as an educator. This is the only legitimate

way to explain how the director knew in March 2015, that I would

need to be moved due to poor test scores.

Giving the director the ultimate benefit of the doubt, that she

was a fortune-telling gypsy and knew the results before they were

released, she still did not have the authority to make a personnel

decision based on the test scores. The Department of Education

explained several issues with the testing and determined it was

not an accurate reflection and most of the data should not be

used. In accord, the Department of Education issued guidance

stating the following regarding the 2015 state testing that the

director referenced as the latest reason for the transfer:

> *For all these reasons: the department determined that tying quick scores to performance levels on TCAP was not a best practice. Indeed, quick scores were intended for use only in calculating student grades. Quick scores should not be used for accountability, with schools and districts relying on these scores to determine if AMO targets were met or using them to make personnel decisions.*

The Director has the power to transfer within the system.

However, that is not an unlimited power. Tennessee law states

that the Director can transfer for legitimate reasons as long as the

transfer is not arbitrary or capricious. Each and every reason the

director has stated for the reason of the transfer is pretextual in

nature and politically motivated. The director herself, even told

me that I had done nothing wrong and my personnel file reflects

that – the only truth she told.

> *"It is better to keep your mouth closed and let people think you are a fool than to open it and remove all doubt."*
>
> Mark Twain

Chapter 5

The Lies that Bind

If anyone thinks he is religious and does not bridle his tongue but deceives his heart, this person's religion is worthless.

-   James 1:26

Each time I saw the fourth district school board member, I thought of Boss Hog and the Penguin from Batman rolled into one person. Boss Hog because of his obnoxious and offensive behavior and the Penguin for his narcissisms minus the formal wear. He was "not the brightest bulb in the chandelier." Or that's the way he appeared to me. The things that would come out of his month and the ideas he wanted to implement at the school were just inane. And the way he treated people was just not right. When he called my brothers and asked to meet with them I am sure their eyes rolled. Thoughts, no doubt, were conjectured up as to what now?

My policy as a school principal was never to tell school

board members how to do their job. In the same respect, I did not want, nor did I allow, board members to tell me how to do my job. If I needed anything to improve the students' learning process or enhance teacher instruction, I certainly would ask. Other than that I thought it best for the school board to manage the system while I managed the school.

After he was elected to the seat of fourth district school board, I asked for three things – make sure our students have what they needed to get the best education possible. I asked him to support our teachers and to look into a building program for our students and community. Our school had grown thirty percent in the past three years and we were at full capacity.

Unfortunately, it seemed the three things I asked for were the furthest issues from his mind. He was more interested in scratching backs, and his favorite backs to scratch were the finance director and director of schools.

Of course, he wanted his back scratched as well. He had an

itch that only they could scratch. His itch – for his wife to have a principalship. Not just any principalship though – but the one I held.

Our students and teachers were let down by corrupt individuals playing politics. The finance director was happy to agree for his wife to become principal. It would send a massage to my family and anyone else that refused to play his games. The director of schools was willing to go along with it as well since the both of them vote on her contract. But she made an attempt to satisfy the director of finance by first moving my wife and then moved her back from fear of the Tennessee Education Association.

She would have gone along with anything they wanted. As already avowed, the two of them voted on her contract and that vote was just around the corner. Also, I speculate she didn't want the news to resurface about her niece, an employee of the school system, that was charged with drunk driving and evading arrest.

The arresting officer's report stated when he approached her car he smelled alcohol and said her (the director's niece) speech was slurred. He observed open beer cans and two boxes of Natural Ice beer in the passenger seat. When asked to exit the vehicle and perform a field sobriety tests, she allegedly said, *"Do we have to do that here on the highway? I'm drunk."* Refusing to take a sobriety test, she was arrested and transported to the county jail. At the jail, she agreed to a breath test which registered an alcohol level of .12. In the state of Tennessee, a blood alcohol content of .08 or greater is considered impaired. She was given a slap on the wrist by the director. Not many people in the school system knew about this as they tried to sweep it under the rug.

I'm sure the director of schools knew this story could rematerialize if the finance director did not get what he wanted. He was notorious for holding things over people's heads in order to force them to do what he wanted. He would not think twice about blackmailing anyone, if it would advance his agenda.

One of my brothers asked the fourth district school board member why he wanted to meet. He told them that there was a lot of talk around town and he wanted to clear-the-air.

"What kind of talk?" my bothers asked.

"You know, about your brother being transferred to another school."

"So do you know why he was transferred?"

"No not really – Well, yes I do BUT I CAN'T SAY," he said tilting his head to one side and squinting one eye like he was trying to figure out what just came out of his mouth.

"You mean you can't say or you won't say?"

"Well I'm not at liberty to say, but if I told you what he had done then you would understand."

"Understand what? Is there something going on we need to know about?"

"Yea, but the transfer will take care of the problem. Now, here is what I need you both to do – trust me on this and everything will turn out ok."

"Trust you? You are asking us to trust you, and you are not giving us one single reason or any information to do so."

"You both know that the finance director has a beef with your brother." One of my brothers later said he got up and retrieved a tissue from the box on the desk and wiped the perspiration dripping from his forehead.

"So why is that, why does the finance director have a beef with him?"

"Well you know. It goes back to the election. Your whole family embarrassed him. He told people he could get you all to vote for his man and you guys supported someone else. Now he feels like he needs to get even, but that's him. That has nothing to do with why I'm here. The fault I have with your brother is poor leadership."

"So he is being transferred because the finance director wants to get even and you feel that he has poor leadership skills."

"Yes. NO, NO, well I'm not sure why he is being transferred. I just know that there are things that shouldn't be done and things that should be done that are not," he said chewing his nails. He retrieved his phone from his cargo shorts that extended well below his knees and checked his messages.

"What are you talking about?"

"I mean, there are things going on that you don't know about. I hope you guys are not taping this conversation," he said as he cocked his head and his eyes swept the entire room as if trying to locate a recording device.

When one of my bothers asked, "What things are you talking about?" He said, "I can't say. You just have to trust me."

"We need to know what he has done. Before we can trust you."

"I can prove that this is the right decision. You know to

transfer him."

"Ok, go ahead. We are listening. "

"You just have to trust me I can't say. And let me tell you something else, I am a true Christian, and I have learned your brother is not."

"What does that mean?"
"Well Christians don't act like he does."

One of my brothers asked, "What are you talking about?"

"Well in my book he is just not a Christian," the fourth district school board member replied, resting his folded hands on his enormous belly.

"If your brother wants to fight this then things will get really messy for him. Rumor around town is he has lawyered up. He needs to forget about suing anyone because he has zero chance of winning. He just needs to accept what has happened and everything will be fine in about six months."

"Does he have a right to know what he has done?"

"That's not up to me."

"So have you talked with him and told him how you feel?"

"That's not my job."

"Did anyone talk to him about concerns before he was transferred?"

"Yes I'm sure they have. They should have."

"Then there would be a record of it in his in his personnel file?"

"Yes. There should be. I can't say anything else. You just have to trust me."

"We need to know what he has done before we can trust you. The director said he was insubordinate."

"Yes that is what he did. Insubordinate."

"So how was he insubordinate?"

"I don't know I guess because he would not do what the finance director wanted him to do, and you have to do what your superiors say," was the school board member's response.

"Yes, as long as what they are asking you to do is not illegal or infringes on your rights," my brother said.

"That's not the way we see it. He has to obey us."

"Even when it violates his rights as a citizen?"

"YES".

"Before You Embark On A Journey Of Revenge, Dig Two Graves."

Confucius

Chapter 6

Vengeance is Mine

It is mine to avenge; I will repay. In due time their foot will slip; their day of disaster is near and their doom rushes upon them."
                    -    *Deuteronomy 32:35 (NIV)*

June 2015

What do you want out of this?

Before I could answer a second and third question was fired at me. Do you want a boatload of money? Do you want revenge? It was almost as if Lady Justice, who stood proud and straight on his desk uttered the words. I felt her gaze through the blindfold she wore, while she waited for an answer.

I said to myself, "Who wouldn't want a boatload of money. And revenge - I guess revenge does give the soul a type of twisted gratification." Staring back at the bronze statue my eyes judiciously fixed on the two-tray scale she held in her right hand.

Corruption overflowed in one of the trays while all the people

that had been harmed or destroyed by the corruption filled the

other. The persecuted individuals hung in the balance while the

scale tipped in favor of corrupt politicians.

"I want justice!" was my reply. "Justice for everyone that

has suffered at the hands of these corrupt people and justice for

what they have put me and my family through!"

My attorney's next question took me by surprise. "What

does justice look like to you?" I thought it was a strange question

because justice is justice. Right? I mean justice is receiving what

you deserve. Right? I looked at Lady Justice once again, hoping

she would help, this time I swear her eyes were closed behind the

blindfold.

Removing his wire rimmed glasses from his broad face

while wiping a bead of sweat from his forehead with the back of

his hand my lawyer divulged, "Justice is open to subjective

interpretation. And the interpretation is usually done by lawyers and judges as they realize the law does not cover all possibilities as it is written."

"Mr. Cosby," the large overweight man who had spent more time behind his chaotic mahogany desk than he had at the gym continued, "You are correct to assume, justice, in a sense, is the notion that people receive that which they deserve. But others' perspectives and viewpoints can and will impact the meaning of *deserve*. If we ask for a jury trial, their concepts or viewpoints can and will be affected by religion, ethics and equity for example. If we don't ask for a trial by jury then the judge's own beliefs and viewpoints come into play."

"Also, you need to understand that more often than not, cases like these never make it inside a courtroom," the out-of-shape man panted. Breathing heavily, he continued, "They are settled out of court." For the next hour he droned on and on recanting similar cases he had won or settled out of court. "And if you are serious about curbing the corruption in your county, then maybe, with the right timing, we can have a negative impact on their school board reelection next year," He added.

The portly, winded attorney told me his fee would be $7500.00 and one third of any settlement and an additional $2500.00 for expenses if I wanted to proceed. I was stunned it would cost so much. I told him I needed to discuss everything with my wife. My desire was that no one would ever go through what my family and I had gone through. So, after much anguish, prayer and counsel, I felt I had no other choice but to take legal action.

Taking on an entire county and its corrupt individuals does not come without consequences. A lot of consequences actually. It takes a lot of time, energy, and money. The aftermath of my actions were nearly devastating to my family.

My actions certainly were not to seek revenge or money. Although I did want the corrupt and deceitful individuals to be exposed and pay the piper. I have learned that we have no right or credentials to pursue revenge. And no amount of money could repair what so many have gone through at the hands of the corrupt, selfish individuals. I felt my family and I had been wronged and I wanted to cast a light on the corruption and roll back the canopy of black clouds that has engulfed our county for so long.

Two lawsuits were filed. The first named the finance director/school board member for interfering with an employment relationship I held with my employer. The suit stated that the defendant, individually and officially as a member of the school board, and finance director engaged in a series of events to interfere with my employment relationship with the school board. The lawsuit also named the director of schools, individually and officially as director of schools, for malicious, willful and wanton tortious interference with an employment relationship that I held with the school board. This suit was also filed as a cause of action for Official Misconduct and Official Oppression. The second lawsuit named the fourth district school board member, individually and officially, as a member of the school board for slander.

The original lawsuit was amended after depositions, to show a pattern of exclusion by the board of education of potential vendors and contractors and the limiting of purchases of goods and services to a select few individual or groups. (AKA friends of the backscratchers).

The amended lawsuit which was in Circuit Court, also reflected possible violations of certain state statutes spelled out in the Tennessee Codes Annotated TTCA), section 5-21-121, 5-21-123, (b) and 5-21-125. Tennessee law states that the finance director cannot exercise his or her power for their own personal or financial interest while conducting county business. The statutes also states that the finance director shall not have the authority to veto the hiring and dismissal of personnel of the various county departments, agencies, or officials or set salaries or determine the needs of such departments.

Furthermore the statutes state any official or employee of

the county, or of any institution or agency thereof, who fails or refuses to perform the duties required by this chapter or fails or refuses otherwise to conform to the provisions of this chapter commits a Class C misdemeanor, and is subject to removal from office or position. The amended lawsuit also stated that the defendants retaliated against me by hiring a forensics auditor to audit the financial records while I was principal for the purpose of swaying public perception and attempted to indict and or prosecute knowing there were no evidence that I was guilty of any wrongdoing.

The negative publicity the finance director received over those two years appeared to have had a damaging impact on his reelection bid. The news about the amended lawsuit hit the local paper just before the 2016 county general election. The people of the six district went to the polls with *Class C misdemeanor - subject to removal from office* fresh on their minds. After the election he only held one position in the county, and that was finance director. His defeat as school board member came at the hands of a well-respected and retired schoolteacher.

> *"The most wasted day of all is that on which we have not laughed."*
>
> Nicolas Chamfort

Chapter 7

Three Things to do Each Day

Bless the Lord, O my soul, and forget not all his benefits,

-Psalm 103:2 ESV

Do not neglect to do good and to share what you have, for such sacrifices are pleasing to God.

-Hebrews 13:16 ESV

Laughter is the sun that drives winter from the human face.

-Victor Hugo

A typical Walmart run – this time for printer ink. I was not in the mood to socialize with anyone. I just wanted to make my purchase and get back home before bumping into someone I knew.

Then-

" MR. COSBY is that you?," shouted a booming voice. For a second I thought it was coming from the PA system. I turned to see a bear of a man headed my way clad in mud caked jeans, a frayed grey t-shirt with *Go Vols!* across the front that had almost faded away. The John Deere cap he wore looked too small for his huge head. He looked as if he had not had a haircut in weeks and a razor had not touched his face in days. I presented my right hand to the man, who towered over me. I knew my hand would more than likely be sore and bruised tomorrow. Ignoring my extended hand, he grabbed me in a bear hug, my feet no longer touching the floor he said, "It is real good to see you. We miss you real bad up at the school."

Back safely on the floor and able to breathe again, I told him, in a breathless voice, it was good to see him as well and asked about the family. He said they were all fine but they did not care for the *asshole* that was now at the school. "He don't care 'bout them kids like you do," he said loud enough that anyone within 50 feet could have heard.

This gentleman had three children at the school while I was principal. He and his wife were big supporters of the school. They attended every meeting and volunteered at the school whenever they could. They always taught their children the importance of an education. They supported the teachers and staff and had a great relationship with every school employee.

"How's things going fer you, Mr. Cosby? Do you need anything?" he kindheartedly asked. I told him I was fine but missed the students. "What them sumbitches done to you was wrong! They need to pay. I hope you jerk a knot in their tail. They deserve what they get," he said not caring who heard his remarks. I thanked him for his words of support and trying to change the subject, I asked him how he was doing. He said he was getting by.

I told him again it was good running into him and that I needed to get home and finish some computer work. I was happy to see an extended hand on his end but knew my hand would need an icepack soon. Shaking hands, he said, "I'm fixin to get some smokes and head back to the ridge." With a half-smile I said, "Those cigarettes are going to get the best of you." He replied, " I reckon sump'n gonna kill us all one day, mine might as well be Winston lites."

"Okay, whatever you say. Tell your wife and the kids I said hello and I miss them."

I turned to leave when he put a hand on my shoulder as he said, "Mr. Cosby, can I show you sump'n?" pulling out his wallet. "Sure," I said. He took out one of my business cards from his wallet. Soiled and tattered it looked as if it had been in his wallet for years. I immediately knew what he wanted to show me, but I didn't know why.

My deepest desire as principal was to see each student prosper and succeed in all areas of their lives. My third year as principal, I started requiring students who entered my office to complete a certain task. Whether they were sent to my office for discipline or reward, they all were required to complete the task. Not just one and done but each time they were in my office they completed the assignment.

After they were rewarded or disciplined or if they just dropped by to say, "Hi," I would give them one of my business cards and something to write with. I would ask them to turn the card over and write on the back - *Three Things to do Each Day*. I told them each and every time that I do these three things everyday myself, and it has made me a happier and better person.

There were times I needed parents to come in and discuss their child's behavior or grades and sometimes both. I would have students write the *Three Things to do Each Day* in front of their parents. I would explain why I felt each of the three actions worked to make better and happier individuals. Then I asked the students to put the card in their wallet, purse or somewhere they would not forget about it. More times than I can count, parents would ask if I minded if they took one of my business cards and wrote the *Three Things to do Each Day*.

Students, parents and sometimes teachers would inscribe on the back of my business cards,

Three Things to do Each Day

1. Count your Blessings Each Day.

2. Find Someone to Help Each Day.

3. Find Something to Laugh about Each Day.

As the cards were being imprinted, I shared with the inscriber how blessings can bring happiness and comfort to us. It is so easy to take God's blessings for granted in the world in which we live today. We are saying and showing that we appreciate what God has done for us by counting our blessings every day.

I have discovered that it is human nature to want more and desire that which we do not have. Counting our blessings each day can take our mind and desires off what we don't have and make us more grateful for the things we do have.

Next I explained how studies have shown that helping others can help keep things in perspective by making us feel more positive about who we are and helps heighten our overall sense of purpose and identity. Some data suggests that when we help others, it can stimulate physiological changes in the brain connected with happiness. I would tell my students, "Just help someone and see how it makes you feel." Experts say that helping others improves our frame of mind and ultimately makes you more optimistic and positive. Now I ask you, "Who wouldn't want to be more optimistic and positive?"

The third thing I encouraged my students to do each day was to find something to laugh about. I cautioned them not to laugh at or make fun of anyone. They knew that was bullying, and it would not be tolerated.

It has been said, *Laughter is the best medicine.* Laughter is a powerful medicine and it has so many benefits such as boosting the immune system by decreasing stress hormones and increasing infection-fighting antibodies making us more resistance to disease. Laughter also releases the body's natural feel-good chemicals called endorphins, which encourages a sense of well-being and can sometimes relieve pain.

I thought at one time it would be nice to share with the school board and see if they would want to practice the Three Things to Do Each Day, but I was reminded of what Mark Twain said years ago; *"In the first place, God created idiots. That was for practice. Then he made school boards."*

When this parent asked if he could show me something, and I saw what it was, it brought back so many memories of students I attempted to help become successful in life. But it was what he said after removing the card from his wallet that touched me profoundly. With tears in his eyes, he said, "Me and my family have had some real hard times the last little bit. Money's been tight and food scarce. My family and me, Mr. Cosby, have been living from paycheck to paycheck. And to make things worser, my hours was cut back last week."

"But I have not let none of this get me down," he said smiling through the sadness on his face. "You know why, Mr. Cosby, that it has not got me down?" Before I could say anything he said, "Cause I count my blessings every morning before I get out of the bed. I am blessed with a good wife and three beautiful and smart young'uns. We have a roof over our heads and a little land, it ain't much but it's airs. I got a job that don't pay much, but it's a job. I could go on and on about my blessings, I have so many things to be thankful fer."

He went on to say, "It don't matter how rough things get, me and my family finds somebody to help. That's why I asked you Mr. Cosby if you needed anything. You know it makes a person feel real good to help someone out." I couldn't speak because of the lump in my throat grew larger and larger so he went on and said, "There have been times that finding sump'n to laugh about has been pretty hard but we always make it a point to laugh at sump'n before we go to sleep at night."

"Mr. Cosby," he said with a voice not as robust now, "These three things on this here card has got me and my family through some tough times and we thank you fer that." He extended his hand for a final handshake, but I ignored his hand and gave him a bear hug – his feet stayed on the floor.

> *"No weapon formed against you will prosper. But make no mistake, the weapon will be formed."*
>
> Christine Caine

Chapter 8

No Weapon Formed Against You Will Prosper

"No weapon that is formed against thee shall prosper; and every tongue that shall rise against thee in judgment thou shalt condemn. This is the heritage of the servants of the Lord, and their righteousness is of me, saith the Lord."

Isaiah 54:17 KJV

News of the lawsuits spread across the county like a heavy blanket of fog over the Smoky Mountains. Everywhere I went people came up to me and wanted to shake my hand and encourage me with the fight I had ahead. They would say things like, *stick with it, thank you, keep your head up, keep up the good work.* They all wished me the best of luck. I was also told to be careful and not to let my guard down.

I remember an elderly gentleman approached me at McDonalds' one morning and said, "You've been around long enough, son, to know how dirty these crooks are. They will stop at nothing to get their way. They will destroy you, so be careful."

Not long after the lawsuits were filed my wife answered a phone call from a lady that wanted to encourage us not to give in to these people. She said, "I know it will be hard on your whole family, but don't let them win." She told my wife that her husband was treated the same way years earlier. She explained that they did not have the resources to fight, and he needed a job; so they had to accept what was done to him.

The strength and inspiration I was receiving from my new fan club waned shortly after the defendants were notified that legal action had been taken against them. That is when the threats intensified. Letters in the mail at first, then phone calls. The letters were anonymous and the caller's or callers' numbers were blocked. Both forms of threats suggested it would not end well for me or my family if we continued legal action. I remember one letter, in particular, in which the writer stated they had a dream that I was in a house engulfed in flames and unable to get out of the inferno. Instead of a signature, the letter ended, *This is a warning*. I do not know if the dream actually occurred, nonetheless I took it as a threat. This went on for eleven months and when it became apparent, I could not be intimidated into dropping the lawsuits things heated up even more.

I could see and feel a storm brewing but I was in too deep. I had invested too much time and money to bow out now. Besides, if I turned and ran from the storm a lot of people would continue to suffer at the hands of these criminals. The next eleven months dark clouds of misery, depression, and fear blew into my life testing my faith and causing me to second guess my decision to fight the corruption.

The person on the other end of the phone whispered, "I need to tell you something, but I cannot get involved in this. If they found out I called you, they will fire me in a heartbeat. And I need my job." I had known this person for years, and a trustworthy relationship had developed between the two of us. I believe this person was honest and had my best interest at heart. They had worked at the district school board office for years and we had mutual respect for each other. I asked, "What now? What's going on?"

"Promise you will leave me out of this."

"I give you my word, what's up?"

"They are planning to set you up."

"Set me up? What do you mean?"

"I overheard the director of schools and two school board members talking this morning. They have someone following you."

All sorts of questions pierced my psyche. *Why would they have someone following me? Set me up? How? Will these people ever stop?*

"They were talking about planting something in your car."

"Was one of the school board members also the financial

director?"

"Yes."

"Are you sure you heard them right?"

"Yes, and I overheard them say when it's in your car an officer would pull you over and arrest you. So please be careful especially since it looks like the sheriff's office could be involved. And always lock your car."

I knew they would go to extreme measures to force me to drop legal action so I really was not surprised at their scheme. My family and I were very careful not to get caught off guard by these thugs. I knew what they were capable of so we battened down the hatches and got ready for the storm.

My mind started to drift. *Could the local sheriff really be involved?*

One evening, a few years earlier, one of my brothers, my dad and my uncle stopped at Hardees for a quick bite before a county commission meeting. We were just finishing when the finance director/six district school board member came through the door. After getting his order of two bacon cheeseburgers and black coffee, he came over to our table and sat down. He didn't ask if he could join us. He just sat his tray on the table and pulled up a chair from another table and sat at the end. "Good evening gentleman, how are the Cosby men this evening?" We said we were fine and asked how he was doing. He didn't answer but asked if we were attending the meeting tonight. We said we were planning on it. He said, "Well you guys are in for a good show tonight. One of the county commissioners doesn't want to do as he's told so we've got a surprise for him tonight."

I thought to myself, *Dinner and a Show.*

He stuffed his mouth full of cheeseburger and washed it down with coffee. "Sometimes a little humiliation is good for people. It keeps them in line," he said wiping ketchup from his mouth with a paper napkin. He winked and said, "I'm really good at starting rumors on people. And if they don't stick, I have friends in high places that owe me favors." He stood taking the orange plastic tray and said, "Enjoy the show tonight," as he dumped the contents of the tray in the trash. I thought what an arrogant….

I was reminded of what my grandmother would say when she came across a narcissistic person. I have heard her say many times, of a self-admiring individual, "I wish I could buy him for what he's worth and sell him for what he thinks he's worth." We decided not to attend the show.

Could the local sheriff really be involved?

The finance director/six district school board member's words years earlier, *I have friends in high places that owe me favors,* rang in my ears.

Over the years the corruption of the county sheriff included kickbacks from illegal poker machines, forgery, tax evasion, a grand jury indictment on charges of sexual assault and statutory rape at gunpoint. He denied the rape charges but agreed to a deal that would wipe his record clean after completing two years' probation. He was also cited by Tennessee Wildlife Resources Agency officers for shooting a deer without a hunting license on county fairgrounds. The sheriff claimed he was going to use the venison for inmates' food. So, yes, the county sheriff was less than honorable, and he could be involved.

After two weeks of looking over our shoulders, I received another call with information about another overheard conversation. "Hey, they were talking a few minutes ago about having your computer's hard drive".

"What do you mean, my computer's hard drive?" Knowing no one would have had an opportunity to acquire my hard drive without my knowledge.

"All I know is they said the tech person went up to the school and got the hard drive from your computer."

My first thought was *why?* Rubbing the back of my neck, I could feel a headache coming on. *My school computer.* It is April. I have not been on the campus since June of last year. That's ten months. I took a deep breath and tried to collect my thoughts. *Why would they want information on my old office computer? What are they looking for?* I knew they would not find anything inappropriate and so did they. *So why do they have it? And why did they wait ten months to acquire it? Were they planning on putting inappropriate material on it and trying to use it for leverage? Surely they would not stoop that low. Would they?*

I could not say that I had not been warned. I was told many times that things would get messy for me and things would not work out for me. Who was I kidding, sure they would stoop as low as they needed to in order to teach me a lesson. I remember saying to my lawyer, "These people are really trying to destroy me!" His reply, "Well, what did you expect? You are exposing them and their evil deeds.".

My inside person called again, this time from a number I did not recognize. "There was a man in the director's office this morning. She met with him for about half an hour before the finance director joined them. I don't know who he was, but your name came up a lot." Who knows what they are up to now. Who cares, but I still asked, "Why were they talking about me? What were they saying?"

"I don't know something about doing an audit on you and your financial records while you were principal."

"Ok fine, let them, I've done nothing wrong or illegal."

The state of Tennessee requires school records to be audited every year, and my school always had good audits. So I wasn't concerned until my inside person said, "I heard the director tell the man, *find something, even if you have to make it up.* Then the finance director said, *you better come up with something as much as we are paying you.*"

"What did the man say?" I probed

"I don't know, he talked low, I could not hear his response. Another thing, the word *forensic* was used several times."

They were talking to someone about doing an audit and the

word forensic was used.

Forensic Audit.

I had heard of forensic audits but I really didn't know what one was. I called my son, who was preparing for the bar, to ask him what a forensic auditor does. He told me this type of auditor examines a business or individual's financial records in order to obtain evidence that can be used in a legal proceeding. He said usually a forensic audit is executed in order to prosecute someone for a criminal behavior.

He wanted to know about my inquiring mind. I told him what I thought the school board was planning. He said he was sure they would not find anything wrong with my records. I thanked him for the vote of confidence but told him about the hard drive and the plan to set me up some way. I hated to lay all this on him as he was beginning to study for the bar, but I needed to see what I was up against.

Knowing how ruthless these people can be and trying to

put a puzzle together with only pieces my informant supplied me was exhausting. I asked my son, "Okay, so what's the worst that could happen here?" There was a pause on the other end, and finally he said, "Dad, if you have your facts straight, and I don't doubt that you do, they will try to prosecute you. If you are prosecuted and found guilty, then you could lose your retirement benefits and possibly go to prison and pay a large fine." I swallowed hard trying to rid myself of the lump in my throat and finally said, "Don't they have to have proof? I've done nothing wrong." I was weary. For the first time I was gripped with relentless fear.

"Dad I know you have done nothing wrong, but I don't have to remind you who we are dealing with."

"Okay, what do we do?"

"We wait, see what their next move is. You asked what the worst thing is that can happen. I told you. That doesn't mean any of it will happen," he said trying to make me feel better and wishing he had not told me.

"Okay, worst case scenario, let's say they try to prosecute me. What do we do?"

"We fight. We get a good criminal lawyer, and we fight. It will not be cheap but we will not have a choice."

"So how much are we talking?"

"Between $40,000 and $50,000".

Wow, I thought. I have already spent $10,000. Now I might have to shell out another $40,000-50,000. Is it worth it? I didn't have an answer for my question.

The next eleven months seemed like an eternity. The days were long and the nights longer. Thoughts of prison, losing my retirement benefits, and embarrassing my family produced an unshakable fear that continued to grow. My mom and dad had taught my two brothers and me the importance of hard work and

a good name. My mom would often remind the three of us of

Proverbs 22:1- *A good name is to be chosen rather than great*

riches, loving favor rather than silver and gold. Although I had

done nothing wrong, the unethical and corrupt individuals were

trying to destroy everything I had worked for my entire life.

I never heard from my informant again. I figured they

found out about the phone calls and somehow their job was

threatened. So I had no inside information as to what was going

on, and that was very agonizing. The fear continued to grow and

grow. Were they still planning on planting something in my car to

set me up? What were they going to do with the hard drive from

my computer? What on earth could they make up in the forensic

audit to get an indictment and to prosecute me? These questions

and others flooded my every thought.

Staring down the barrel of the unknown, a paralyzing fear

began robbing me of joy and freedom while emptying my

emotional bank account. I wrestled for the reins of control, while misery emerged with a vengeance, spiraling me into a deeper and darker depression. I begin realizing I cannot do this much longer. I have to turn loose of the reins. I am no longer in control. Was I ever in control? When I stopped grasping for the reins and turned them over to God a dam of tears broke loose.

Standing in my living room on June 21, 2016, I started praying. I told God I couldn't do this anymore. I can't fight this battle. You have to take this burden from me. The weight is just too heavy, and I have no more fight in me. I was not sure how God would respond to my pleas. I did not know how He would deliver me from my enemies. Would it be through scripture? Would He give me a sign? Would He send a message through someone? Would He speak to me in a small still voice, like He did Elijah? Any of these responses would have been fine with me. I was desperate and needed to know God was there. I needed him to take the reins of the situation. Actually, I needed Him to take the reins of my life.

God doesn't do anything halfway. He never has and never will. He spoke to me that day in a clear, distinct voice, "I have been here waiting for you. All you have to do is trust me." I was to the point I had nothing else to offer but trust. I was at my breaking point.

God also sent a message through my wife, who was in another room praying for the threats and harassment to end. Shortly after God spoke to me, she comes into the living room, where I was learning to trust God. She puts her arms around me and says, "Everything is going to be okay. This will soon be over." I asked her, "How do you know?" She shared with me how God led her to Isaiah 54:17. She said God revealed to her the audit, a weapon that the enemy had formed, would not prosper. She said, "They will not be successful in what they are trying to do to you."

For most people, God speaking to them in a clear, distinct voice, saying to trust Him, would have been enough. Sending a second message through a loved one, that everything would be okay, would just be icing on the cake. However, God knew I needed a third message. That night I had a dream. I dreamed I was alone in a place I didn't recognize at first. When I got closer to the edge of the road, in the ditch, I saw three dead horses.

> *"God blesses you so that He can do for others through you; it is not always about you."*
>
> D.A. McBride

Chapter 9

It is Not Always About You

...but to those who are selfishly ambitious and do not obey the truth, but obey unrighteousness, wrath and indignation.

- Romans 2:8

My phone alerted me of a text. Then another. I poured my second cup of joe and checked who was texting so early. It was my nephew, Justin.

Are you home?

Would you mind if I dropped by in a few?

Sure what's up?

I need to get your opinion on something.

K

I grabbed my coffee and my phone and headed for the deck to enjoy the sunrise with Wrigley, our family's black lab - named after Wrigley field in Chicago because of my son Tyler's love of the national pastime in honor of the historic and hallowed field.

I settled in a comfortable wicker chair, Wrigley on the floor by my side, to appreciate and relish in God's artwork. As the sun's first rays peaked from behind the ridge, the clouds progressed from a gray smoky color to a warm red and orange shade. God's canvas stretched from one end of the sky to the other with the colors becoming more brilliant with each passing second. I'm not sure which Wrigley enjoyed most, the sunrise or his head being scratched. I would assume the latter.

His perked ears let me know someone was in the driveway. As the family canine jumped to his feet and ran to meet our guest, I go inside to refill my coffee cup and pour a cup for Justin: his cream with two sugars, mine black. Returning to the spot I had witnessed God's display of beauty just a few minutes earlier, I watched Wrigley escort my nephew up the sidewalk.

"You are stirring early this morning," I said offering him the lighter shade of coffee. "Yea, I have a project due in a couple of days for school, and I thought I would spend some time at the library to finish up," he replied thanking me for the coffee. I invited him to sit and enjoy what was left of the God's masterpiece.

"I guess you heard David backed out of running for school board in the 4th district," he said rubbing Wrigley's head.

"Yea, I heard. I hate that. He would have made a good school board member. I suppose they got to him like they got to the others.

"They threatened his wife's job. He said she was a cook at one of the schools and they couldn't do without her income."

The corruption never ends I said to myself. While several people wanted the fourth district school board member gone, no one wanted to get involved because of the repercussions of standing up to the corruption. Three different people picked up the necessary paperwork to be on the ballot. All backed out. I suspect their change of heart was due to threats made to their families.

Justin took a sip of coffee and placed the mug on the wicker side table next to where he sat. "The reason I am here is because I wanted to get your option on who we might get for a candidate," picking up the coffee mug again and taking another swallow. "You know Justin, I say let's not worry about it. Yes, I would like to see him out of office; but I'm tired, and I think I would like to just stay out of this election." I excused myself to get refills, feeling bad for not wanting to get involved myself.

I returned with cups in hands, my nephew seized his caffeine – cream two sugars. He smiled and said, "What do you think about me running for school board?" I returned to the wicker chair, stepping over Wrigley. I sat my coffee on the side table placing my right hand on my forehead trying to think of the right response to his shocking question. I did not want to hurt him, so I finally said, "Justin don't do this for me. It is okay, I'm fine." He takes a long sip of coffee and said, "I'm not doing this for you, I'm doing it for the students and teachers."

The silence was deafening! The next few seconds felt like an eternity. I tried to hide my embarrassment while Wrigley seemed to be taking in every word – at one point I swear he put both paws over his eyes to hide from the awkwardness of the moment. The only thing I could think to say was, "Okay then, it looks like we have a candidate for school board in the 4th district."

That weekend my son, Tyler, my two brothers, Mike and Mitchell, and Justin met to plan the *Cosby for School Board* Campaign. Of course we sought our father's advice and he requested only one thing; run a clean campaign with no mudslinging. Although we had a truckload to hurl, we would honor our father's request.

After the necessary paperwork was summited to be placed on the ballot for the 2016 election, Justin became an official candidate for school board. He also became a target for the corrupt politicians that wanted their puppet candidate to remain in office. He and my brother were threatened and harassed for months. My nephew was told that he would never work in the county if he did not withdraw his name from the race. My brother was also told if Justin did not withdraw from the race our whole family would regret it. We will investigate your brother and the school records, and we will make sure we find something to send him away for a while. I have to admit, that unnerved me. Not because they would find something illegal but because they would make something up if they had to.

My nephew approached me and said he was planning on backing out of the race because he didn't want to put me through anymore hassle. I reminded him that he was not doing it for me in the first place, so I encouraged him to stay in the race.

Over the next five months he was contacted by various individuals, some offering money, others advice, and some offering both. The fourth district is rural and spread out, so it took a lot of time and money to cover.

The advice and concerns he received involved personnel and taxes. Some wanted someone hired or fired and their taxes not raised. Justin always listened to them and told them he was running for school board to make things better for students and the teachers. He also shared with them that the school board members were not responsible for raising taxes. He told everyone that his goal was to help attain the best possible teachers and work hard to make sure students got what they needed for a good education.

His campaign was a roller coaster ride for the entire family. The threats intensified, but the response he received from voters was very positive. The 2016 general election, the same election that wounded the finance director/ex sixth district school board member, awarded my nephew a decisive victory. A victory for the students and teachers.

> *"There is but a step between a proud man's glory and his disgrace."*
>
> Publilius Syrus

Chapter 10

House of Cards

Pride goes before destruction, and a haughty spirit before a fall.

-   Proverbs 16:18

Queen

The director of schools did not seek another contract extension after 2017. Did her decision have anything to do with the Tennessee comptroller findings in the Financial Audit Report for that year? The comptroller exposed that $7000 was paid to the director of schools without documented approval by the school board. The finance office provided the auditors with a letter signed by the chairperson of the Board of Education, which stated that the board had met on June 5, 2017 and unanimously approved this payment as a bonus for services rendered. However, no board minutes were provided documenting that the June 5th meeting occurred or what may have been approved at that meeting.

It also appears someone tried to hide the $7000 from the public by reflecting it in the teachers' salary line-item in the General Purpose School Fund, rather than the line-item used for the director of schools' salary as reported in the audit. The comptroller recommended that the school board decide whether the money was appropriate. If not, he said the funds should be recovered. The school board, however decided not to pursue litigation to recover the funds. It was reported in the local newspaper legal action was not pursued apparently due to the cost of going to court. **More back-scratching.** Also the school board amended the minutes in early 2018 to show approval of the $7,000 to make it legal, months after the money was paid out.

King

After the finance director/sixth district school board member was wounded in the 2016 election by losing his school board seat, he took another hit in the 2018 election. Both his puppet-mayor and sheriff were soundly defeated. Two factors played a role in their landslide defeats. First, the puppet-mayor, sheriff and finance director pushed for a jail expansion.

The expansion would have cost our county over two million dollars while we are still paying for the current jail. The county really did not need the expansion, especially at a two million dollar price tag. The voters, not wanting their tax dollars wasted on an unneeded jail expansion, voted the mayor and sheriff out of office. Second, the Tennessee Bureau of Investigation raided the sheriff 's office, three months before the election.

The sheriff, along with two other employees of his office were arrested on a myriad of allegations. The sheriff was charged with seven counts of official misconduct, five counts of tax evasion and one count of forgery. One of the sheriff's employees was charged with official misconduct. The other, the jailer, was charged with three counts of a felon in possession of a firearm. Yes, you read that correctly - the jailer was a convicted felon.

Although the sheriff maintained he was innocent and being set-up, the voters did not buy it.

With the finance director's puppet-mayor gone as well as the director of schools, he became uneasy about losing his power and position as finance director. The knock-out punch came when the new finance committee voted 6-1 to relieve him of his duties as finance director. The county commission supported their decision.

Joker

The fourth district school board member's reelection bid came up short. My nephew carried every precinct and won the election by a landslide. For me, it was a bittersweet victory – I was glad the corrupt school board member was gone, but I did not want my nephew thrown into the fray. I also did not want him trying to avenge what had happen to me.

Then I remembered him telling me that he was not running for school board because of me, but for the students and teachers. Again, I was embarrassed but happy. Happy that the students and teachers would have someone in their corner and someone that would not mistreat them. After the one-sided election the former school board member continued trying to force doors open for his wife to become principal. But to this day that door remains closed.

> *"Life is a succession of lessons which must be lived to be understood."*
>
> Helen Keller

Chapter 11

Lessons God Taught Me in the Storm

Lesson One

Forgiveness is not optional – Matt. 6:15 – Mark 11:25

Show me Your ways, O Lord; Teach me Your paths.
-Psalm 25:4 (NKJV)

Forgive them?

FORGIVE THEM!

Are you kidding me? No Way! They tried to destroy me!

They made their brags. They told everyone that would listen, that

I would be indicted. They were going to see to it that I was

prosecuted, spend time in prison, lose my retirement, and drag

me and my family through the mud.

They falsely accused me. All because I stood up to them.

All because I tried to expose their corruption. Their immorality.

Forgive them? Not in this lifetime! It will be a cold day at Satan's address before I would give them the time of day.

They tried their hardest at all levels, holding nothing back to try and prove I committed a crime. They sought to destroy my livelihood and life. They even alleged I was not a Christian.

If you forgive someone, are you not condoning their behavior? Are you not allowing that person to get away with sin? Forgiving someone is a sign of weakness. Right?

Besides that, you don't know what all I've been through! You just don't u n d e r s t a n d !

Did I just say that?

Did I just tell God he didn't understand?

As I began to weep, I could feel God's arms cover me like a warm blanket on a cold winter day. He said, "You are wrong my son. I do understand. I understand that the same powers that controlled the actions of your accusers also controlled the actions of My Son's accusers."

The same "Powers."

Powers?

What *"Powers?"* I don't understand. My accusers were

the corrupt individuals of our county that would stop at nothing if

someone stood between them and what they wanted.

For our battle is not against flesh and blood, but against the
rulers, against the authorities, against the world powers of this
darkness, against the spiritual forces of evil in the heavens.

-Ephesians 6:12 HCSB

God says, our battles are not against flesh and blood.

When we are attacked, when we have conflicts, those struggles

are not from human beings.

Let that soak in for a minute.

Our struggles come from rulers, authorities, the world

powers of this darkness, the spiritual forces of evil in the unseen realm. In other words, Satan and his demons.

Jesus understood this as he was falsely accused and heard the crowd shout to the top of their lungs, "Crucify him!" The same people he had fellowshipped, worshipped and eaten with just a few hours earlier, now wanted him dead. Jesus understood this as his skin was being ripped from his back while the Roman soldiers repeatedly beat him. Jesus understood this as the Roman soldiers spit on and mocked Him. He understood and knew the powers that made the soldiers shove a crown of thorns into his scalp and continue to strike Him in the head with each blow, driving the razor-sharp thorns deeper and deeper.

Jesus understood this as he walked the narrow cobblestone street to His death. With each step blood gushed from his back and head. Carrying a 100-pound piece of wood that would become His cross, people pointing His way and covering their mouths. Some laughing, but most in disbelief. Jesus understood this as nails were pounded into his wrists and feet.

Weak from the blood loss and dehydration he uttered -

"Father forgive them for they know not what they are doing"

And I had enough audacity to tell God He didn't understand!

Shame on me!

I am the one who did not understand!

I did not understand that my misery was coming from holding grudges, and not wanting to forgive my enemies. Also believing that forgiving those who hurt you is a sign of weakness. Friends, that doesn't hold water.

"Father forgive them for they know not what they are doing"

"But I say to you who hear, Love your enemies, do good to those who hate you."

Luke 6:2

No, it is not easy and you cannot do it by yourself. I had to first want to forgive those who hurt me if, for no other reason, than to free myself from the heaviness the came with the misery. Once I decided to forgive, I had to ask God to teach me how to forgive. It was impossible for me to forgive on my own. I needed God to transform my calloused heart into a forgiving one. Over time and with a lot of prayer I was able to forgive them. Understand that I am still a work in progress, but now misery free.

Lesson Two: Our identity is in Christ, not in a position.

"Therefore, if anyone is in Christ, he is a new creation; old things have passed away; behold, all things have become new."

2 Corinthians 5:17

Twenty years of being pulled in a hundred different directions every day. Someone always wanting something, meetings to attend, paperwork to complete, deadlines to meet, ballgames, bus duty, fire drills, on and on and on. Now everything had changed. No one was wanting anything. No one was needing anything. My organized chaotic days were uneventful now. I missed it.

I used to be the person in charge. The person everyone went to. The person with all the answers (so they thought). The PRINCIPAL, that's who I was. Now that no one was coming to me for anything, I felt lost and without a purpose. The very foundation of who I thought I was had been shaken to the core. It was during this time that God taught me I had misplaced my identity.

Somewhere along the way my identity had become my career as a school principal. A position that I loved but had allowed it to consume my life. When it was all gone, I didn't know how to act. I didn't know who I was. I didn't recognize myself. Depression had incarcerated me in a jail of sadness, discouragement and hopelessness. I felt no one needed or wanted me any longer. I felt as if I no longer belonged anywhere.

While sadness, discouragement, and hopelessness held me prisoner, God spoke to me through His Word. As I turned to Scripture for answers, I was led to Paul's story and his identity crisis.

In Acts 9:4-6, God shared with me how Paul's misplaced identity, as a zealous crusader against Christians and a despiser of the Gospel shifted to his true identity as a writer and speaker of the truth when he met God on the road to Damascus. Even though the Apostle Paul struggled with his identity, he is considered to be one of the most influential leaders in the Christian church, sharing the gospel of Jesus to Jews and Gentiles alike. He also, penned a large portion of the New Testament when he discovered his true identity. Paul's example reminded me that our true identity is in Christ not in a position. When I finally realized who I was in Christ I was no longer a slave to sadness, discouragement, and hopeless. My true identity also opened my eyes to what was really important in life, the things that I had taken for granted for so long. Our relationship with Jesus, family and true friends at the top of the list.

❧

Lesson Three: Trust Calms Fear

Trust in the Lord with all your heart, and do not lean on your own understanding.

Proverbs 3:5

I felt alone and afraid. Fear's grip was so tight, at times I couldn't breathe. The choke hold it had on me got tighter and tighter with each passing day. My fear was so palpable it began to affect my health. Day after day of wondering what was next. I think I felt like David when he wrote, *"My heart pounds in my chest …. Fear and trembling overwhelm me, and I can't stop shaking. Oh, that I had wings like a dove, then I would fly away and rest"* - Psalms 55:5-6 *(NTL).*

I did not know the results of the audit or if it was even

completed. The waiting intensified the fear. The unknown, the sleepless nights, the thoughts of "worst case scenario.". The auditor never contacted me throughout the entire investigation. I did hear from multiple sources that they tried everything in their power to put together a case against me. They attempted to involve authorities at the highest levels, but in the end they found no criminal intent.

I knew this because the director of schools and the two soon-to-be lame duck board members sent me messages that said, *You were warned and you did not listen. You only have yourself to blame for what you will be facing soon. The TBI and district attorney both say they have enough to indict you and the Tennessee Comptroller's Office will soon be contacting us.* I couldn't tell if this was another warning or just them crowing.

I knew that the Tennessee Bureau of Investigation, the Tennessee Comptroller's Office and the DA's office are all respected and honest organizations but what I didn't know was what lies and misrepresentations the forensic auditor would create.

The auditor was told, according to my informant, they had better find something for the amount of money he was charging. During depositions the director of schools admitted that the audit cost over $33,000 of taxpayers' money. A lot of money to stop me from trying to expose their deeds. Makes you wonder what they were really hiding.

The realization that I could lose my retirement, my name, and everything I worked for was more than I could handle. The gravity of it all pulled me down to my knees. I remember praying to God, "I can't do this anymore. It's too big for me and I don't have any more fight in me. You have to take this from me and whatever your will is may it be done." It was then I heard God say, "I have been here waiting for you. All you have to do is trust me."

I had nowhere else to go and trying to handle this on my own was not working. When I decided to get out of God's way and trust Him to handle things for me, fear relaxed the grip it had on me. There were days that I still struggled with the unknown, but I was reminded of David again and what he wrote in Psalms 55:16-18 - "But I will call on God, and the Lord will rescue me. Morning, noon, and night I cry out in my distress, and the Lord hears my voice. He ransoms me and keeps me safe from the battle waged against me" (NLT).

When I turned everything over to God, He showed me in a dream that powers that used to rule over me would soon be powerless.

Author's Note

The breathtaking beauty and the hardworking, honest people of our county make it an amazing place to live and raise a family. Although the clean and refreshing air of our small town can sometimes be polluted by the immorality, manipulation, and fraud of corrupt politicians, it is still the place I proudly choose to call home. Not all elected officials are sleezy and corrupt. In fact, we have a lot of good, decent people that have held and presently hold elected offices. I am not naïve enough to believe that the corruption I stood against was unique to our county. I know it extends far beyond our county and the only way to fight it is through prayer and sometimes taking a stand.

I am reminded of a quote from Winston Churchill, "You have enemies? Good. That means you've stood up for something, sometime in your life." I do not enjoy having enemies, but I take comfort in trusting my actions made a difference in others' lives.

The old country store which was a gathering place for the community during my childhood is no longer standing. But the storehouse of memories made there, remain a part of us.

Made in the USA
Middletown, DE
21 April 2022